ACTION
IN THE
MOMENT

ACTION
IN THE
MOMENT

*Self-Awareness and Intuition for
Leaders in Ambiguous Times*

Thomas G. Swenson, Ph.D.

ARCHWAY
PUBLISHING

Archway Publishing books may be ordered through booksellers or by contacting:

Archway Publishing
1663 Liberty Drive
Bloomington, IN 47403
www.archwaypublishing.com
1 (888) 242-5904

Because of the dynamic nature of the Internet, any web addresses or links contained in this book may have changed since publication and may no longer be valid. The views expressed in this work are solely those of the author and do not necessarily reflect the views of the publisher, and the publisher hereby disclaims any responsibility for them.

Any people depicted in stock imagery provided by Thinkstock are models, and such images are being used for illustrative purposes only.
Certain stock imagery © Thinkstock.

ISBN: 978-1-4808-2954-1 (sc)
ISBN: 978-1-4808-2955-8 (e)

Library of Congress Control Number: 2016905061

Print information available on the last page.

Archway Publishing rev. date: 4/18/2016

Note:

i The symbol on the book cover is an Arabic Numeral that can be found in G.G. Neill Wright's The Writing of Arabic Numerals (Publications of the Scottish Council for Research in Education, Volume XXXIII), 1952.

This book is dedicated to my wife.
Without her love and encouragement,
this book would not have been written.

CONTENTS

ABSTRACT

"Action in the Moment" presents self-awareness and intuition as key concepts in developing a model of individual and organization behavior where ambiguity is the foundation of reality. The world around us is not clearly right or wrong. Everything appears to be gray with no clear meaning or obvious direction for us to take. In any situation that involves human behavior, we do not know the outcomes of interest and/or we cannot measure the outcomes. Nevertheless, we must still make choices. Most of us sense that something is wrong, very wrong.

> *"Man must not attempt to dispel the ambiguity of his being but, on the contrary, accept the task of realizing it."*
> -Simone de Beauvoir (1947)-

The assumption of uncertainty as the basis of reality is very wrong when we live in an ambiguous world. Various philosophers, psychologists, behaviorists, scientists, mathematicians, quantum physicists, politicians, artists, poets, and athletes are among those who provide examples in support of ambiguity as the basis of reality and the importance of self-awareness and intuition for making decisions whether in our personal or organizational lives.

"I believe in intuitions and inspirations …
I sometimes FEEL that I am right.
I do not KNOW that I am."
-Albert Einstein-

Collectively, we have studied almost every aspect of organization behavior and in spite of all the effort to improve our understanding of individual and organization behavior we have little to show for it. We have some good slogans, and yet, we have ended up with just as many problems as ever.

In this book, I have attempted to turn our thinking around and look for answers in ourselves. My position is that we should admit that ambiguity is fundamental to our existence, become more self-aware, celebrate risk taking, fearlessly enter the unknown, and develop our intuitive leadership potential. We do not have the time to take the easy way out by thinking of reality being based on uncertainty and allowing probabilities to run our lives. We clearly have much to do.

It is time for a paradigm shift in how we make decisions. We need to develop an understanding of how to find patterns in the chaos and take "Action in the Moment."

This book is thought provoking and encourages a conversation about the assumptions we make about reality, and how important self-awareness and intuition are in responding to the apparent chaos presented by ambiguity. At least, we need to recognize that we really cannot know much about our own behavior until we understand the reason we exist and take action in the moment. I hope that the perspective presented will stimulate others to continue the development of a new paradigm for understanding human and organizational behavior.

Do not dwell in the past,
do not dream of the future,
concentrate the mind on the present moment.
-"Buddha"-
(As cited on URL http://www.brainyquote.com/
quotes/quotes/b/buddha101052.html)

INTRODUCTION

This book identifies self-awareness and intuition as key concepts for building strong social systems in ambiguous times. In the past, uncertainty has been the basic assumption for problem solving and decision making for individuals and social systems. Uncertainty has been the basis for understanding the world around us.

However, when it comes to human behavior, uncertainty is not the basis of reality. The result of relying on uncertainty as the dominant paradigm for problem solving and decision-making has failed. Behavioral research spanning one hundred years can claim to explain only ten to twenty percent of the variance in human behavior.

Ambiguity is a much more reasonable basis for our thinking about reality and for making decisions in the real world. The world around us is trying to tell us something as we find ourselves living in an ambiguous world where there is no black or white. Everything appears to be gray with no clear meaning or obvious direction for us to take. Most of us sense that something is wrong, very wrong.

We are not just confused about what to do; we are like the deer frozen in the headlights of an oncoming car. We are not self-aware enough to drag ourselves from the quicksand that seems to be swallowing us. Indeed, it is not only that we have become incapable of making decisions, we have also lost track of who we are.

This book presents a new paradigm for studying all types of social systems. Whether it is individual, family, organization, community, national, or global levels the dominant paradigm that relies upon problem-solving analytics based on uncertainty and decision theoretic in explaining all forms of human behavior has failed. I will argue: why ambiguity should be the basis of reality, how self-awareness provides the critical insight into the values that provide the meaning of our life, and discuss the importance of intuition for taking "Action in the Moment," in developing viable social systems.

Social systems simply do not have the resources to leisurely study a situation, develop a plan for solving a problem, evaluating alternatives, and implement the plan. Behavioral systems of all types are under great pressure to act first and then make any needed modifications. Do not look for guidance in the past. You have to identify patterns in the chaos and quickly take action in the moment. The pressures on organizations to adapt to changes in the marketplace and intensive competitive forces demand lightning fast decisions and action.

Collectively, we have studied almost every aspect of human behavior and in spite of all the effort to improve our understanding of behavioral systems; we have little to show for it. We have some good slogans, and yet, we have ended up with just as many problems as ever. In this book, I attempt to turn our thinking around and look for answers in ourselves.

We are told to: empower ourselves and others, build strong social systems, communicate better, develop flexible infrastructures, and intrinsic reward systems, create strong cultures and identity, encourage risk taking, allow more discretion in judgment, improve emotional quotients, use out of the box thinking, think globally, encourage innovation and learning, lead with integrity, and become visionaries.

You would think that with all of this well intended coaching we would not have any problems at all. Well, we do have problems and many of them. We seem to be tossing slogans around without being able to explain these concepts except by relying on other abstractions. At a time when we seem to be continually moving into the unknown, where time is of the essence, we still do not have anywhere near a robust understanding of human behavior. When you consider the growth in the human development book market you can see that satisfactory answers are not being offered.

Well, there is a better way. The answer may be found by: changing our assumptions about reality, acknowledging ambiguity in the world, realizing the importance of self-awareness in understanding reality and human behavior, understanding how ambiguity allows free will, and realizing that intuitive reasoning is the preferred decision-making methodology in ambiguous times.

I hope the perspective presented will motivate further development in our understanding of human behavior based on ambiguity being the basis of reality. This book focuses on a specific subset of all human behavior. It will present the importance of self-awareness and intuition to the study of organizational behavior.

Although it focuses attention on organization behavior, the reader should keep in mind that the conceptual understanding presented has application to any area of human and social behavior at all levels of study. A graphic overview of the book can be seen in Figure 1. It provides a conceptual mapping of the book that may be helpful to building a systemic understanding of the concepts presented in this book.

Others have endlessly considered all of these concepts. This book provides an understanding that begins with a fundamental change in the assumptions we make about reality. This is why the book begins with a consideration of the question "Why do we exist?" The answer to this question presents a fundamental change in the way we think and make decisions and the concept of free will and self-awareness.

The importance of self-awareness is available in the literature (Tjan, Harrington & Hsieh, (2012), Brooks, D. (2015)). However, there is little consideration of how we can develop our self-awareness and intuition or why self-awareness and intuition are important. It is at this point that I make a connection between ambiguity, the insight provided by self-awareness, and the foresight provided by intuition. In tandem, self-awareness and intuition provide the basis for making decisions and taking "action in the moment" in these ambiguous times. You may find figure 1 helpful to refer to periodically as you read the rest of the book.

FIGURE 1
GRAPHIC OVERVIEW OF THE BOOK

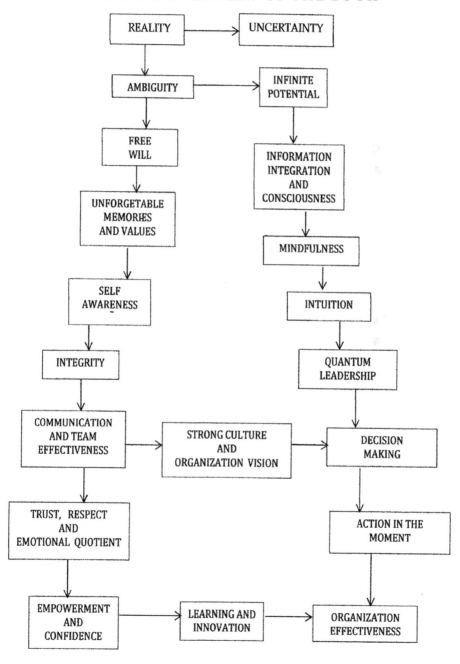

REALITY AND WHY WE EXIST

A paradigm shift this extreme needs to start by asking a basic question: Why do we exist? Our existence is both individually and organizationally relevant. Philosophers have been studying reality for a long time. The discourse has involved two basic assumptions of reality: the determinist with uncertainty as the basis of reality, and the modernist with ambiguity as the basic assumption of reality.

For the longest time, we in the West have been under the influence of pure reason. The meaning of life is a machine metaphor. It is time to create new forms of meaning. We have witnessed for too long the most devastating effects of the rationalist/determinist assumptions that threaten to enslave humanity with an unquestioned set of externally controlled codes, which create our reality. The law of reason is no longer acceptable but has actually become a barrier to the discovery of truth and meaning in our lives.

UNCERTAINTY

The most dominant assumption that has formed the basis of reality is uncertainty. Under conditions of uncertainty the outcomes of interest are known, measurable (reliable), understood, explainable, and controllable. Behavior under conditions of uncertainty is a walk in the park compared to ambiguity.

It is simply much easier to consider situations where uncertainty is the presumed reality. For example, when attempting to study any human behavior, we are much more likely to assume that we know the outcome we are studying, such as organization effectiveness, and we can actually deceive ourselves into thinking we are actually measuring organization effectiveness.

When we find the factors that are significant in predicting organizational effectiveness, we will inevitably believe we have improved our understanding of and even possibly our ability to explain organizational effectiveness and consequently adopt strategies to control what we think is organizational effectiveness.

This occurs all the time despite the fact that we do not know if we are measuring effectiveness or even capturing a significant portion of the ultimate criteria. The ultimate criterion captures the total longitudinal value to all of the organization's stakeholders. It is easy to see that it would be impossible to measure the ultimate criteria. (See figure 2).

FIGURE 2
ERRORS INVOLVED IN THE MEASUREMENT
OF THE ULTIMATE CRITERION

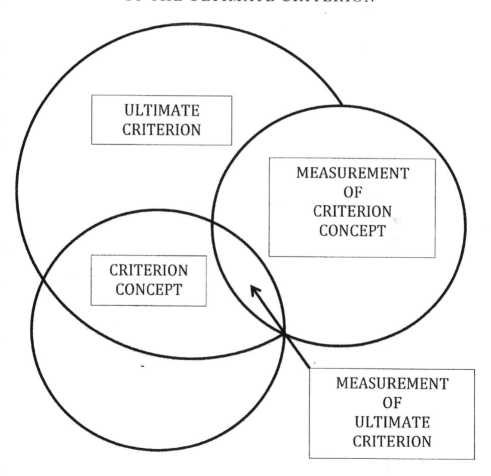

It is amazing how many interpretations of research results ignore a discussion of the limitations the operational measures used in their study. This deficiency exists for both criteria and predictor measures.

When you do not know what you are measuring, the results will certainly defy interpretation.

Another deficiency in relying on uncertainty-based research paradigms is that the results typically look across subjects but not over time. The subject's changing mental models are ignored. We refuse to change our minds based on new information and other deficient measures. None of these methods eliminates the bias introduced by the measurement deficiency inherent to research on human behavior.

Just think for a moment what this means if, when dealing with human behavior, the outcomes of interest were truly known, measurable (reliable), understood, explainable, and controllable. If the reality of human behavior was based on uncertainty, a machine could replace us and there would be no reason for our existence.

This is the harsh truth of how we have endeavored to understand our reality. Yet we have still managed to convince a great many people that our results (mental models) represent the true reality. It may be that we shy away from utilizing intuitive means of making decisions to limit any personal responsibility for a mistake made by intuitive means.

The concept of uncertainty is not actually the problem I have with a method for seeking "truth"; it is more an issue with measurement (Feibleman, 1962). Do we really know what we are measuring? Our "models" of any result or outcome are only as good as our measurements. The operational measurement we use is where I have my problem. The greatest bias comes from how quickly we accept such poorly constructed operational measures when it comes to the understanding of human behavior.

We have collectively accepted uncertainty as truth to the exclusion of almost any other principles guiding our lives. We are introduced early in elementary school to decision-making methods collectively known as the scientific method. Uncertainty is the basis of the scientific method. Elementary school may have changed over the years, but you never hear anyone talking about their children coming home talking to parents about ambiguity.

AMBIGUITY

O ne reason we try to avoid ambiguity is that, almost by definition, it is nearly impossible to define. Many definitions of ambiguity are quite ambiguous themselves.

No wonder we do not know much about ambiguity when we could not even define it, let alone teach anything about it. When confronted with ambiguity, we just declare that the situation is complicated and continue our lives based on principles of uncertainty. Use of the analytical left-brain is continually reinforced.

The following serves to illustrate how little we know about ambiguity.

Merriam-Webster defines ambiguity as "The quality or state of being ambiguous, especially in meaning" and "A word or expression that can be understood in two or more possible ways."

No wonder ambiguity seems scary! We are incapable of defining ambiguity, let alone building curriculum and methodologies to teach it. Maybe we could develop better definitions by looking at some of the synonyms for ambiguity.

Suggested synonyms for ambiguity are obscurity, darkness, equivo-calness, equivocation, inscrutability, inscrutableness, murkiness, mys-teriousness, obliqueness, obliquity, and opaqueness. Most of these synonyms should be on a list of the most difficult words to use in a sentence. These definitions and other descriptors for ambiguity just do not help.

I think my definition of ambiguity is more useful, particularly when considering human behavior and the outcomes resulting from human behavior. I define ambiguity as a characteristic of situations where the outcomes of a decision are not known, or the results of a decision or action cannot be observed or measured, or the outcomes can have two or more possible meanings (Frost, 2002; Holbeche, 2011; Kruks, 2012; Byers, 2010).

What follows are some situations that illustrate much of what I am talking about when I refer to the concept of ambiguity. Consider the following examples:

Faculty Grade Distributions

The first example occurred when I started university teaching. I dis-covered that there was an annual report on each professor's grade distributions over their previous year of teaching. These published re-ports received considerable attention from students and faculty alike.

I was sitting in the faculty lounge one day with a few other professors perusing the report when the discussion turned to the professors who had handed out the highest grades and those who handed out the lowest grades. What followed was a discussion of the meaning of high-grade and low-grade faculty.

It quickly became apparent that high grades and low grades were viewed as both good and bad. In fact, the teachers who had flunked the most students were given great praise by some for maintaining high integrity in their evaluation of student performance and simultaneously criticized by others for being a terrible teacher because so many students had flunked their courses. The same information was seen as being representative of good teaching and bad teaching. How could this happen?

I stayed out of this discussion but was an attentive observer, and I have often found myself involved in this discussion throughout my career. This argument continues, in one form or another, at probably every university in the world to this day and will probably continue forever because the judgment of a student's performance is, by any measure, ambiguous.

All of you who have attended a university have had at least one professor who you believed could not teach anything to anyone but for some reason had received promotion and tenure and was the only teacher who taught a course in your degree that you could not avoid. Of course, every university needs to have at least one teacher who has no hesitation flunking a student.

I was always confused in this discussion because, since a student could usually drop a course they were flunking, I could not understand why a student would stay in such a class unless they never knew how they were performing in the class. My position generally resulted in an end to the conversation because if students knew they were failing, they would drop the class and the distribution of grades would then be biased in the direction of passing grades. This discussion continues among faculty and administration and will never be resolved.

Again, it is a problem with measurement because the professor's grade distribution is a poor measure of effectiveness. Who among us, as students, hasn't had a conversation with other students in a class regarding a professor's grading tendencies. Everyone wanted to know what professor was an easy grader in every course. In fact, the university administration often publishes a report with their names and distributes it campus-wide.

The easy A professor might actually be the best teacher at the school. They may have even decided to jeopardize their tenure by ignoring the publishing requirements for tenure and spend their time developing their teaching abilities. Therefore, the best teacher may be fired and the search for a replacement begins with the numerical count of juried publications being the most important criteria for identifying the best candidate. (Note: I personally believe that a good professor should actually aim for all of their students to get an A.)

Of course, it is equally possible that the professor simply gives high grades because they have become tired of the queue of students outside their offices complaining about the grade they received. Therefore, they might actually be the worst professor at the school from the standpoint of achieving the course's learning outcomes but do not want to be bothered by the student complaints regarding receiving an "F" or even a "B." Unbelievably some students have never received any grade but an "A".

I could give many other examples of how academic systems and their outcomes are ambiguous. I am also sure that you too could offer many of your own examples of how ambiguous reality is in academics. It is not uncertainty that defines reality. When it comes to human behavior, of any kind, the reality is more correctly considered ambiguous.

Newspaper Headlines

Whether in formal meetings or water cooler discussions we have found ambiguity slipping into the conversation. Ambiguity is often found in the newspaper headlines. Newspaper headlines provide excellent examples of ambiguity. Headlines also demonstrate how useful ambiguity is in humor. Just a few examples of ambiguity in newspaper headlines follow:

Iraqi Head Seeks Arms

Prostitutes Appeal to Pope

Teacher Strikes Idle Kids

Miners Refuse to Work after Death

Juvenile Court to Try Shooting Defendant

Red Tape Holds Up New Bridges

Typhoon Rips Through Cemetery; Hundreds Dead

Man Struck By Lightning Faces Battery Charge

New Study of Obesity Looks for Larger Test Group

Kids Make Nutritious Snacks

(As cited on http://www.fun-with-words.com/ambiguous_headlines.html)

Comedians Love Ambiguity

One humorous example I still find very funny is a classic joke of George Carlin's (unless he stole it from someone else). In the joke, Mr.

Carlin draws attention to a glass, which was half filled with water and asks the question "Is the glass half-full or half-empty?"

Of course, both are correct, but Mr. Carlin in his unique style takes it one-step further and states that he was confused because he thinks, "a better answer is that the glass is too big." The greatest comedians are very good at pointing out alternative realities.

Although these are humorous illustrations of ambiguity, they do provide us with a reality check. The following is another very contemporary and contentious issue that is useful to our understanding of ambiguity.

The U.S. Constitution

The second amendment of the U.S. Constitution is loaded with ambiguity. "A well-regulated militia, being necessary to the security of a free state, the right of the people to keep and bear arms, shall not be infringed." There are different types of ambiguity presented in this amendment:

1) "Right of the people": is it a collective right or an individual right?
2) "Keep and bear": does this include, bringing a pistol to school?
3) "Arms": does this include, say, surface to air missiles or RPG's?
4) "Infringed": does licensing qualify as infringement?

Is there any wonder that it has become almost impossible to reform gun laws? It is not bullheadedness alone. Ambiguity plays a huge role in all of our lives and so does the constitution.

Perhaps it is time to admit that ambiguity changes everything and it does not make life any easier. Ambiguity is inevitable and ubiquitous and it did not happen just yesterday. Ambiguity has been around for a long time and found to be very useful for a variety of purposes. The Tower of Babel might be just around the corner, or, maybe we have already arrived.

If we accept ambiguity as the essence of reality and the reason for our existence, we are actually able to exercise our free will. Moreover, I think most people would say that free will is a good thing. The line separating good from bad is almost nonexistent. The machine metaphor for our existence clearly separates good from bad.

General Considerations of Ambiguity

When we say to someone, "Have a nice day, can we know what nice is"? If not, how could we observe a nice day and then how could we understand or affect the outcome of someone's day? Is it possible to measure any conceptual abstraction in the study of human behavior? We have apparently convinced ourselves that we can do just that and careers are made convincing others that they have measured a conceptual abstraction.

Consider the following:
Do we know what organization effectiveness is?
Are we able to measure the effectiveness of human performance or team performance?
Do we know how to evaluate health care?
What is death with dignity?
Do we know what communication effectiveness is?
Is the use of drones in warfare good?

Is gun control good or bad?

Is immigration good or bad?

Is rapidly increasing profitability, good or bad?

Is spanking an unruly child good or bad parenting?

We have all answered these types of questions, without much thought of their ambiguous nature. If we are honest with ourselves, none of these types of questions could be answered using the scientific methods.

If we cannot measure an outcome of interest, what is it that we are predicting and does it help our understanding when we do not know what we are measuring? Alternatively, have we created a façade to hide the inadequacies in our reasoning?

If these questions could be answered in a valid manner, there would be no reason for our existence. Think about it. If a machine was designed to observe and measure the degree to which behavior of any kind did, in fact, occur it would be a simple matter of designing a machine, which could replace us. The machine would not just be a metaphor for reality it would be the reality.

I for one believe, there is a reason for our existence and the reason is not for us to develop a machine to replace ourselves. It seems that uncertainty, as the basis of our reality is much scarier than if we accepted ambiguity as its basis. At least with ambiguity, there is a reason to exist. Additionally, with ambiguity we have free will and choice (machines do not make conscious choices) which provides us with the abilities to identify creative and innovative decisions and perhaps even a better personal and work life. Mechanistic free will is indeed an oxymoron.

Acknowledged experts in the domain of artificial intelligence come close to concluding much the same when they state that a critical question in the area of artificial intelligence is "what is the question, the answer to which is, what is the question? This acknowledges the difficulty of embedding learning into a machine intended to model consciousness and human intelligence.

The key ingredient to learning, particularly creative, innovative, improvisational learning is free will and self-awareness and not externally dictated operational rules. Can a machine improvise? Well, when it does we typically conclude it is broken and quickly go about fixing it even though it may not be broken.

Therefore, if we can accept ambiguity as the condition of our existence, then, everything changes. Ambiguity, choice and free will, changes everything. The probabilities become almost useless when dealing with any aspect of human behavior. Experientially derived guessing (gut feeling) might be just as good as or better than any probabilities derived when elements of the past and future are constantly changing. Second order probabilities and fuzzy set theory simply will not work when the outcomes of interest cannot be measured.

The techniques we were taught to solve problems are perhaps useful when dealing with closed systems where you can come close to observing, measuring, and controlling the outcomes. However, even when considering the hard sciences, there is always some remaining amount of ambiguity in our measurements because we cannot observe or measure something without affecting what we observe.

Moreover, if we accept that we always affect what we measure, we also, cannot know how much we have affected what we have measured. Reality is like unset Jell-O, and we mold the Jell-O to our liking. There is a relatively obscure story from Greek mythology that is useful to illustrate this point. The story describes a wealthy nobleman named Procrustes, whose name means "he who stretches". He kept a house by the side of the road where he offered hospitality to passing strangers, who were provided a pleasant meal and a night's rest in his very special bed.

Procrustes described the bed as having the unique property that its length exactly matched whosoever lay down upon it. What Procrustes did not tell the stranger was the method by which this "one-size-fits-all" was to be accomplished.

As soon as the guest lay down Procrustes went to work on them, stretching them on the rack if they were too short for the bed, and chopping off their legs if they were too long. There seems to be a good deal of stretching and chopping going on today as one's ideology fights another for control of reality.

Our research too often is much like this story in that we tend to make our research decisions regarding what to measure, how to measure, who to select as subjects and when to measure the variables used. All too often, we have found the truth to be the result of this Procrustean Effect. Ouch!

Life is about not knowing, having to change,
taking the moment and making the best of it,
without knowing what is going to happen
next. Delicious ambiguity …
- Gilda Radner -
(As cited on https://www.goodreads.com/author/quotes/145047.Gilda_Radner)

The Spin Doctors

No discussion of ambiguity would be complete without some consideration of the ways that ambiguity is used as an important tool in different professions. Some professions have found ambiguity quite useful. Politicians, attorneys, advertisers, sales persons, and even ministers are among many, that have become experts in the use of ambiguity in persuading others of something for their personal benefit (unintentionally, of course). Have you ever listened to a politician speak on almost any topic, and after they were finished, you have absolutely no idea what the politician said. This technique of "ambiguity-speak" has provided many a politician with that all important "plausible deniability."

In almost any setting, fifty percent of the audience attending a political speech walks away thinking the politician supports something and the other fifty percent thinks the politician opposes whatever the issue might be. Everyone walks away thinking that the politicians agree with them and will receive their vote.

Politicians have raised the use of ambiguity to an art form and the results have been full employment for the spin-doctors. I expect to see a new degree awarded at universities called Doctor of Spin with a major in Ambiguity and a specialty in Rhetoric.

Advertisers are also among some of the best at using ambiguity for their own professional ends. Consider, frequently used terms today, such as, "free." For most of my life, I used to think I knew what "free," meant. However, now I have to read the fine print to determine if free is now on the spin charts.

In recent years, I cannot tell you how often free cost me money. In fact, now with all the internet business connections and charging techniques available I think there must be endless renditions of free. I think that some organizations may actually have some form of an R & D department for researching "free" as a dimension of pricing. You often do not even know who is charging you what money for things you thought was free. Caveat emptor is very much alive and well in business today. The pricing decision in marketing has to include how to convince the customer that the product is free.

Again, we just have not learned much that is useful for sorting out the truth of something under ambiguous conditions. We have tried to build models of our understanding of all sorts of things. It can be estimated that our best models of human behavior can only explain at best 20% of the variance in behavior (and I am being generous). This limited explanatory power of our models ignores limited statistical significance. They still have great utility in decision-making because of the practical significance of reducing the cost of error. However, when we rely on cost reduction as our method for accepting a particular model we may be wondering down a path that leads us away from the truth and to the "land of greed and corruption." At least, one might wonder how "utility" can be determined when the outcomes cannot be measured.

Our current methods for problem solving do not provide us with much confidence in predicting or understanding human behavior. Of course, even if we get close to modeling some outcome of interest, the spin-doctors are always there to spin the outcome to mean something very different from intended. Spin is a cancer and probably a pre-existing condition for which we need supplemental insurance coverage. We might even be able to blame Obamacare for almost anything that goes wrong. I better call my insurance agent and see if I am covered.

Of course, the insurance companies have large numbers of attorneys, who, I think actually discovered ambiguity. At least, the process of justice and the resultant case law interpret values and meaning. However, the case law has only led to more questions regarding truth and justice.

We are all very aware of the failures in our mechanistic, bureaucratic world and the results of simple minded, blind acceptance of rule based organizations. Since our current understanding of behavior is a deception based on the scientific methods that we were taught, we are actually living a lie. When we discover the lie, we will eventually find some way to tell the lie in another way (the spin) until it is accepted as truth and we begin all over again.

Actually, we unknowingly find ourselves trying to respond to our ambiguous world by becoming ideologues. Again, politicians have come to our rescue and provided us with a model of this method for coping with ambiguity. We often hear political issues debated on an ideological basis and we find ourselves agreeing or disagreeing strictly on labels. We live our lives by ideological labels and seldom search for personal truths.

Our human nature leads us to protect these ideologies. We can get very anxious and defensive when confronted with ambiguity. Unfortunately, this condition simply leads to more ambiguity and cliché based decision-making. If you have any doubt about ideologies being a crutch, just consider the toxic nature of the 2016 campaigns for President and the use of the ideological label to convey truth.

Free will permits these differences and creates the diversity that we actually may need to grow as a civilization. We are free to believe the way we chose even when we have surrounded ourselves with clouds of spinning lies to avoid all truths. Life is so delightful that we have to fight for our beliefs or someday, someone may impose their beliefs on us.

Life is indeed quite the conundrum. Maybe it is time to look for ways to solve this conundrum, or, at least, acknowledge that life is a puzzle and everyone needs to find their truth and untie their own personal Gordian knot of existence.

SELF-AWARENESS

Encyclopedia Britannica defines self-awareness as the "Conscious knowledge of one's character, feelings, motives, and desires." It is the ability to self-reflect on the many levels of consciousness within which we exist. It allows us to reflect and navigate effectively, the physical, mental, emotional, and spiritual realms of consciousness that allow us to bring balance, serenity and focus in the midst of chaos.

Self-awareness includes the ability to evaluate the strengths and challenges of our personalities, the ability to understand and recognize our emotions and the impact they have on our equilibrium and the impact that they have on others. Additionally, self-awareness is prerequisite to the use of intuition as a guide to our decision-making and building a sense of clarity and self-worth.

If we are stretching our understanding of the known, we will be reaching into the darkness of the unknown and the unknown is always ambiguous. My position is that learning and intellectual growth are desirable and ambiguity is what we encounter along the way. If we do not know who we are and do not have the confidence and courage that comes with being self-aware we may find ourselves looking for the comfort of the accepted known and hiding from the unknown.

We would no longer be viable or capable of responding to situations for which we were not originally designed. We need a moral compass.

We do not want to find ourselves like a deer frozen in the car's headlights. Just like the deer, we need to act and act quickly. To confront the unknown we need to develop self- confidence, the courage to act and learn from the results, and possess the basic skills and knowledge needed to make sense of our experience and avoid any negative unintended consequences that, if we continue on our current path, would surely result in some form of a collapse of civilization.

We must become intensely self-aware and self-awareness is a process that requires continual attention. (Jelinek & Litterer, 1995; Marques, 2006; Lynn, 2004; McKeown, 2010). However, do not worry too much, there is hope, and it is very close. It is in each of us. It is in our individual memories and intuition is in our collective memory. Values are expressed in every experience and define the importance of the memory. More precisely, values reside in our memories.

Our most salient values are not just in any of our memories. Our important values are in our most important unforgettable memories. In addition, the important memories are those we cannot forget even if we tried. We savor these unforgettable memories because they are important and they are important because they identify the most highly valued experiences that provide us with our awareness of self. These memories also provide us with a filter for viewing the world around us and discovering patterns and meaning in the apparent chaos.

This may be where we can find the basic coding of our existence. These memories are those that contain great passions. We feel proud or, perhaps ashamed of these personal experiences. This is where we might find our core values that we could use to evaluate alternatives, take action, and measure the results, thereby enabling us to discover patterns of meaning that eventually form our intuition.

The values embedded in these memories provide us with our moral compass, our own moral imperative to navigate in this ambiguous world.

To identify these lasting memories, it is useful to ask yourself the following kinds of questions:
- What decisions or actions do I regret making?
- When did I feel most inspired?
- When was I the saddest?
- When did I feel real joy?
- What actions made me feel proud?
- What memories make me feel most alive?
- What memories give us strong feelings of guilt?

It is important to note that some of these memories may bring about extremely negative feelings. With the memories that have negative connotations, you need to consider the positive values that are in opposition to the negative feelings. My point is - focus on the positive values and not the negative. Negative memories do not mean you are a bad or evil person or that you are destined to be evil. Remember that the opposite end of the negative is the positive. All of these unforgettable experiences are expressions of who we are.

These memories are not just the kind you can remember. No, they are the memories that you cannot forget. For some reason, they are very important to you. Remembering these experiences brings on powerful emotions. You feel as though you would be a different person if you did not have these experiences. These experiences are inspirational. These values provide: a guide for future action, your reason for being, the reason for your existence, a primary focus for action, and the patterns of meaning that define our reality.

These experiences contain a value template for action when confronted with ambiguity. They are the instructions for living and you wrote them. These memories provide you with a sense of home. They provide you with a profound set of values that make you self-aware and can be used to judge all the alternative behavioral options available to solve a problem.

You will find that you feel no guilt or difficulty explaining your actions when these fundamental values guide your action. It is useful as a code of conduct that defines who you are and will lead you to where you want to be. In this regard, it becomes a personal vision "to act in a manner consistent with who you are." It is this code of conduct for action that will always place you where you want to be. Identifying these values is crucial to your visioning process and, can be used in the development of a vision for a family, community, or organization.

UNFORGETTABLE MEMORIES

Some examples of these kinds of experiences might prove useful at this point. The following are a variety of my own personal, unforgettable memories and the values that I have found within them:

Grandparents' Kitchen Pantry

This is one of my earliest experiences and memories. I do not think I was more than two or three years old. I remember crawling into a kitchen cabinet and simply looking around. I was in the kitchen pantry. It was a relatively dark place with the smell of paper grocery sacks and wood. I was totally at ease with absolutely no fear of the unknown. After considering this memory and why I retained this memory above all the early childhood experiences, I realized the feeling I had, might best be called innocence. Upon further consideration, I determined that the foundational values of these feelings of innocence included trust and respect. I trusted my instincts, even at that young age and had a great respect for my surroundings and the people in it.

I respected my parents and grandparents that they would never have let me, explore like this unless they did not think it was important for me to extend my limits, and explore this before now unknown territory, fearlessly with complete confidence. My sense of discovery was definitely unforgettable and actually probably set me on a track toward an entire life of exploration and learning.

This was the earliest memory of my sensing the world around me. It was extremely vivid. I explored with all my senses and I was fully aware of discovering something outside of myself as I innocently explored this unknown. I was creating my own reality. It was not just the experience itself, but how I experienced it with the innocence needed to reach into the unknown and to know no limits to learning. Trust, respect, confidence, exploration, discovery, and innocence were acting together like a breath of fresh air after gasping for the next breath of life that would provide still another memory.

U.S. Marine at Attention

This experience occurred when I was teaching at the Naval Postgraduate School in Monterey, California. Part of my responsibilities included a requirement to chair thesis committees. One of my U.S. Marine students was involved in writing a critical chapter in the writing of his thesis. One, Friday he came to my office and asked if he could use my office computer to work on finishing his thesis. I said, sure and wished him well in his writing over the weekend. Monday morning I arrive at my office to find this same student in uniform at full attention outside my office door.

I thought this was a bit strange and I asked him why he was in uniform and why at attention. He was apparently very concerned about something and he stated that he had accidently reformatted my hard drive over the weekend and erased all of my work. Class notes, research, papers, correspondence were all gone. He ran out of disk space on his floppy and was in the process of formatting another diskette when he inadvertently formatted my hard drive instead of his floppy. I had come close to doing the same thing once or twice myself.

The next thing he heard me say has definitely effected who I am. Quickly, without hesitating, I found myself saying, "It was no problem because if whatever was erased was really important, I would be able to reconstruct it and, anyhow, the second time would probably be better than the first time I wrote it. I walked into my office and never mentioned it again. I saw a relieved expression fall over his entire body. WOW! I am sure he was relieved, but I was peacefully delighted with what I had done.

I had experienced what I have come to know as immediate forgiveness and I have used it many times on some very complex problems that needed to be resolved quickly and there was no reason and/or time to spend on blame.

It allows you to rapidly move through the blame phase and immediately get to work on solving the situation at hand. No more huffing and puffing, ranting and raving and your employees can always count on being treated in a dignified manner, no matter what. It also sends a very strong message to subordinates that you did not want them to hide problems. All I wanted was for them to do their best, and do not take the results too personally. Just learn from your mistakes, grow, develop, and move on to the work of improving the total system.

I have always been proud of my use of immediate forgiveness and most who have worked with me will tell you they have grown in many ways because of this principle. I did not realize it, but my understanding of self was also changing and I was growing.

Trip to a Muslim Village in Vietnam

This memory involved me taking a group of very privileged students from the United Arab Emirates to Vietnam on a Business Opportunity Tour. I wanted to expose them to the early stages of economic development and the emergence of a struggling middle-class as they simultaneously dealt with various forms of corrupt practices.

Well, the trip went very well. The students indicated that the fog of business concepts finally made sense. They were able to experience raw economic opportunities and improved quality of life. In addition, there was one memory that stood out from all the rest. I felt it would be worthwhile for our group to visit a village that was comprised of Vietnamese Muslims. I will never forget this portion of the trip and I doubt if any of the Emirate students will either.

We arrived at the village unannounced, not knowing what we might expect. However, there was an immediate connection between the students and the villagers once the students started speaking Arabic (the language of Islam). The students saw the poverty in the village, their compassion for these villagers was leaping out of their hearts, and they asked to see their school and mosque. We were told the village had no school or mosque and only one, rather worn Koran.

The students immediately made a commitment to pay for the building of a school and a mosque. This visit did not last more than about 30 minutes at most. However, the students have, over time, returned to build the school and mosque and provide other support to improve their quality of life. These students learned and reinforced in me, the importance of compassion, human dignity, and sharing.

A Young Man Sheltering a Dying Dog from the Rain

One of the most profound memories I have is a time when I was driving my car on a very rainy day. As I was on my way to somewhere, I do not recall where. I saw a young man, in his early 20's kneeling down beside a dog that he had picked up off the street after the dog had been run over by a car. It was apparent, that the dog was dying. The young man took off his raincoat to shelter this poor suffering animal from the driving rain. This young man's soul was caring for this animal as the dog was suffering during its last moments of life.

This was an indelible memory of how powerful compassion can and should be. Providing comfort to those who suffer may be one of the most important things we can do to express a sense of our own selflessness. Acting in a compassionate manner is perhaps the best way for us to feel, very deeply, how unimportant we are and how connected we are to each other.

The preceding stories are shared as examples of my own unforgettable memories. Some of your stories may be similar to mine. All of these memories provide a very real sense of the importance of the values that make us who we are and are a reminder of how important emotions and feelings are in our lives. They also provide a strong statement of how inspirational our values are to who we are. These are the powerful feelings we experience when we become self-aware.

THE VALUES ARE HIDDEN IN THE MEMORIES

Now you have to identify the values that give these experiences the meaning to your being. (Cady, Wheeler, DeWolf, & Brodke, 2011) These memorable experiences will not always clearly express the values that define them. It may also be useful to allow plenty of time to explore the deeper values hidden in the memories. These values will become the ultimate criterion we can rely on for evaluating solutions to problems or making choices under ambiguous situations. So, take your time to think about the foundational values that make the memories profoundly important to you. You are on a path toward a more enlightened understanding of the reason for your existence. You are waking up.

The following provide examples of how deeply values may be hidden in your experiences. Values that define your unforgettable memories are not always easily discovered. They are often deeply hidden behind superficial values.

Here are some examples of what I mean:

1) Consider a time when a teacher praised you as a standout performer because you identified a unique solution to an assigned problem. You

might say that the value was, learning, but the deeper value might be more along the lines of play, curiosity, imagination and creativity. Moreover, even deeper values might be trust and respect. Ultimately, you are the one who will have to decide the meaning of your unforgettable experiences. I only suggest you take your time. You will know when you have dug deep enough.

2) You might have a memory of a child at play, which brings a tear to your eye because, over the years, you had lost your innocence. If you dig beneath the value of play, you might discover that the value is really innocence. It might actually be youthful innocence or genuine joy. The deeper values here might also be trust and respect. It may also be that the ultimate message is to not take things too seriously.

I have many memories that seemed anchored by learning. However, when you look deeper in the memories, you will find the values of trust and respect. There are generally entire networks of value that you may not initially detect. It is like peeling an onion the outer skins may be innocence, play, curiosity, courage, human dignity, compassion, imagination, confidence, risk-taking, and discovery, but as you go deeper, you may find the underlying values are such as trust and respect.

Do not just scratch the surface keep on digging deeper and deeper. You can see that the meaning or value of a memory might be different the deeper you dig at understanding why a memory is important to you. The important thing to remember is that the meaning of the memory comes from you and there is no rush to judgment. Also, do not discard the outer layer values because they too have a role to play in defining who you are.

Another helpful technique is to write all the values on a blackboard or on a sheet of paper and draw, lines between the values that add meaning to your understanding of the values and help in identifying a network of values that you may not have noticed before.

These are samples of memories that have helped me identify true meaning to my life. It also demonstrates how useful I have found it to write down the memories because it helps to clarify the values embedded in the memories.

Take the time to let these memories wash over you. Do not try to force yourself to remember. Simply, take time to reflect on the values that define who you are. In addition, let these memories flash before your mind's eye. When you finish writing down these unforgettable memories, the easy part is done. You have identified your essential memories. I should note that you are probably never finished identifying the memories that make you who you are. More memories come to mind over time and you create memories that help refine who you are.

Value-based decision-making is generally considered as being important to business and society in general. Nevertheless, they have provided no guidance on how to identify our values. What I have provided is a process whereby your unforgettable memories express the values of who you are. There is a way to discover the values that form your being and it does not require some exotic form of meditation.

Unfortunately, many have opted to let others identify their values. Others persuade us, that values like profitability, wealth acquisition, greed at the expense of the environment, winning at all cost, weapons of mass destruction, win, win, win, technology for technology's sake, or other values that would seem to be destructive as opposed to constructive. It seems we are hopelessly drowning in the values of wealth, greed, violence, suffering, and winning at all costs.

INTEGRITY

Certainly, there will be times that being true to yourself may seem as though you have failed. Let me explain what I mean with another story. Between 1994 and 2005, I was fortunate to have had a number of opportunities to travel internationally as a teacher, consultant, researcher, and entrepreneur. The real story was not about my teaching and business efforts. The real story involves my getting to know and understand a number of people and their cultures.

I was able to meet with and to various degrees, get to know people who lived on the bleeding edge of the rapid early economic growth in developing countries in the Middle East, Southeast Asia, Central Asia, Commonwealth Countries, and Southern Asian. I taught and worked with and sometimes for top U.S. and foreign government officials, including Ministerial government officials and former prime ministers, venture capitalists, expat university professors from various cultures, priests, nuns, ministers, Buddhist monks, the poor and underprivileged, orphans, beggars, the privileged high Mafia and the not so privileged, but feared, Low Mafia youth gangs.

It was almost a continual adrenaline high that was difficult physically and emotionally. It was very easy to feel like a failure if only because I never felt prepared for what I was experiencing and did not know how to define success and certainly was not getting rich or celebrity status.

This sense of failure abruptly stopped due to something a student told me toward the end of this time of globetrotting in my life. What he said to me one day has profoundly influenced my life since. We were visiting one day with not much to do and he said to me Dr. Tom, I do not know how you do it? What do you mean? He said, don't you know? I said, no. He said Tom, you treat everyone the same. You are the most genuine person I have ever met. You treat gang members the same as you treat the highest government official. You do not prejudge others. You do not use the typical stereotypes people expect. You need to know how many people admire you for this. They may not tell you, but you bring a breath of fresh air to others.

Actually, at the time, this caught me totally off guard. I realized that this young man had placed all the memorable experiences I had during this time into perspective. He had helped me to understand that when you act with integrity (Beebe, 1992; Mangham, 2004; Dalla Costa, 1998) you are always a success. No matter what others may think or whether you receive any recognition at all. The truth resides with you acting in the moment, consistent with the values that form your self-awareness.

Clearly, we might benefit from totally changing our thinking. Yes, make no mistake, it will be difficult to make ethical decisions and act with integrity. Nothing worthwhile is easy. However, is it going to be worth the pain? It all seems a bit like trying to run in quicksand. Moreover, there is good reason to feel uncomfortable with what I am saying because it is dealing with the unknown. If we are growing, we will be confronted with unknown outcomes, unknown measures, unknown meaning.

We are reaching into the darkness of the unknown and touching something and we do not have any idea what we found. The dissonance of enacting a set of values that do not represent who you are has created full employment for various types of counselors and therapists. We live in a world that appears to be filled with hypocrites. Finding a person with integrity is quite rare.

It is ignoring ambiguity and the failure to consider the importance of self-awareness that has created our problems. Once you are self-aware, it is increasingly difficult to betray who you are.

It is at this stage that we become consciously aware of our being in relation to our environment and our values provide us with the free will to choose among available alternatives. Without self-awareness, there is no free will and no realization of the why of our existence? Another way is to consider self-awareness as a navigational system that enables you to make choices or simply when you make choices to act in a manner consistent, with whom you are. When you make choices that are consistent with your values, you will always be where you want to be. You will be delighted with your decisions and action. There is no need to explain your actions in terms of what others think. You are your own guide through life. You can now listen to your soul because you make the rules. See Figure 3.

FIGURE 3
SELF-AWARENESS TO INTEGRITY

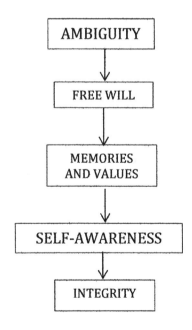

I had always thought that self-awareness occurred at a relatively early age like seven years old. Nevertheless, I have only recently become self-aware of who I am within this ambiguous world. We have sufficient experience to appreciate the value of the experiences. If we did not appreciate the value of our experiences, we would not have remembered them. Remember, the reason you remember something is because you attach great importance to it.

THE FOUNDATION OF
ORGANIZATION SUCCESS

Research has found that self-awareness is the basis of communication effectiveness, team effectiveness, confidence, courage,
risk taking, intuitive leadership, strong culture, creativity, learning,
innovation, continual improvement, and organizational effectiveness.
(Fang, & Wang, 2006; Graf, 2005; Gloor, 2006; Thorpe, 1956; Buck,
2004) Self-awareness is vital to understanding almost all the outcomes
studied in organization behavior and organization theory.

Almost nothing good, in an organizational sense, happens without
self-awareness. Self-awareness does much of the heavy lifting in organizations. It is indeed the backbone of today's successful business and
businessperson. What follows is a discussion of the key relationships
which determine overall organizational behavior.

COMMUNICATIONS EFFECTIVENESS

Self-awareness becomes the foundation for effective communication.
Self-awareness becomes the basis for the identification of overlapping
frames of reference, and improved encoding and decoding. This leads

to the elimination of self and others Deceit that negatively influence communication effectiveness.

See Figure 4.

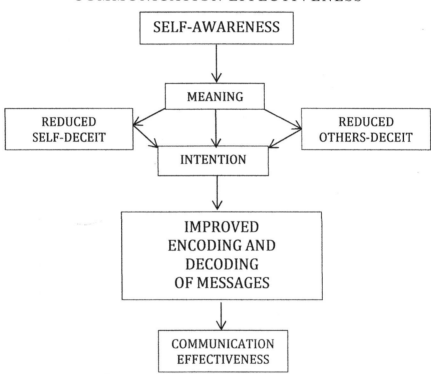

FIGURE 4
COMMUNICATION EFFECTIVENESS

We cannot expect to communicate effectively if we do not know who we are or who others are. In addition, we cannot know others if they do not know who they are. When we are not all self-aware and share our self-awareness by communicating at an experiential level there can never be an elimination of self and others deceit in our communication. Also, there will always be a lack of an overlapping frame of reference, and conflict within the organization will inevitably develop.

It is in this tower of babel we find ourselves today. We have ridden the slippery slope to the betrayal of self. We feel shame for acting not as ourselves. We have lost face.

TEAM EFFECTIVENESS

Self-Awareness in conjunction with Communication Effectiveness will improve the entire team building process. Knowing who you are and sharing that understanding with others, along with, others knowing who they are and sharing this with you, leads to Role Clarity, simplified Goal Setting and the Identification and Enforcement of Norms. Essentially, a great deal of ambiguity associated with another's behavior can be removed when you know more about yourself and others, and, others know more about you.

Everyone has a much better idea of what their role is, what the team's Goals are, and how the team creates and enforces the normative behaviors that are important to Team Solidarity and ensuring Team Effectiveness. See Figure 5.

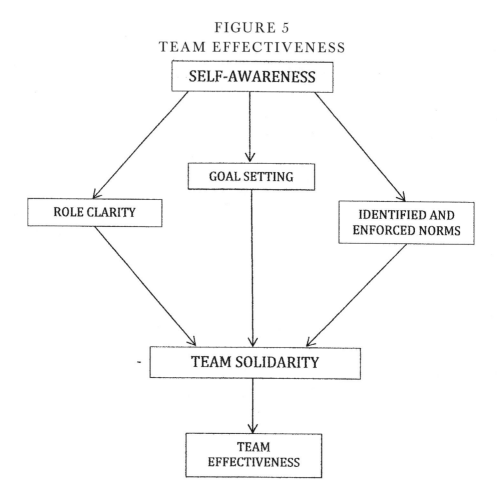

FIGURE 5
TEAM EFFECTIVENESS

There are few decisions made in organizations that are not made by teams. There is strength in numbers and there is nothing like working in a team that is purring along on automatic and operating, as in athletic jargon, "in the zone." You have eyes in the back of your head. You know what everyone is doing and you all have your eye on the prize. Team effectiveness is mainly a matter of trust and respect, integrity and inspiration. The lack of trust and respect is a poison to any team's survival.

EMOTIONAL QUOTIENT

One important result of self-awareness is the raising of your emotional quotient. The EQ is seen by many as being more important, for most people, than intelligence in becoming successful. Integrity follows directly from the improved emotional balance achieved with self-awareness.

Trust and respect are necessary to the integrity that others see in you and what integrity you see in others. The values of trust and respect flow from the process of self-awareness. Trust and respect are a consequence of becoming self-aware, which is the key to all the resultant organization outcomes. See Figure 6.

FIGURE 6
TRUST AND RESPECT TO
ORGANIZATION EFFECTIVENESS

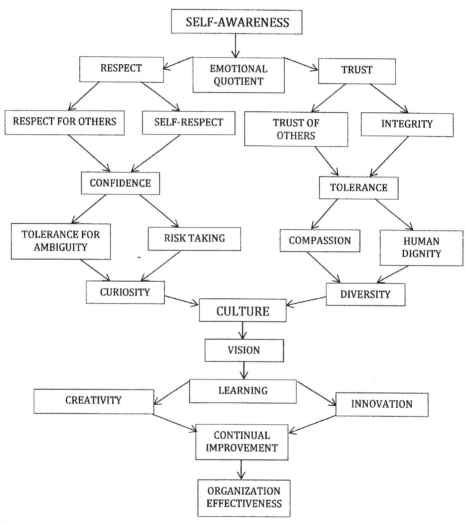

Trust and respect leads to everyone feeling empowered to make the discretionary choices needed in rapidly changing and hostile competitive environments. This empowerment provides everyone with the courage and the needed willingness to take risks to get out of the box in order to transform the organization through empowerment. Everyone has a risk muscle. You keep it in shape by trying new things. Your risk muscle loves to exercise. If you do not, it atrophies.

Now that we have discovered the self, we now have our inspiration. We may now passionately live our lives to the fullest extend and we will always know what to do. .

Others will know why we act the way we do and they understand that if we are acting in opposition to who we truly are, then, when confronted by this inconsistent behavior we will change. Others can actually help ensure that we are living our reason for being. Moreover, we can help others discover their being so they may share with others and we can help ensure they are living their life, self-aware.

The culture of the organization unfolds as we all enact our newly found and shared self-awareness. The leader can mold an organization with others who are inspired by the leader's vision for the company. Truly visionary people and organizations are distinguished by a high degree of emotional intelligence, which requires self-awareness and others' awareness. Whatever decisions you make, will be with you professionally and personally for the rest of your lives and the impact of your decisions will leave a legacy behind you.

The visionary leader's influence is not clearly understood. However, one thing for sure is that others have an improved understanding of the organization's vision and the values embedded in the vision. In fact, the visionary leader is the guardian of the organization culture. Others in the organization look up to this leader as the role model that exemplifies the organization's reason for existence.

As the follower pursues organizational goals and the visionary leader provides the necessary example and resources to do so, the follower becomes empowered and the culture grows stronger. The visionary leader must not betray the organization's vision. They have become the sustaining force of organizational culture.

EMPOWERMENT

Risk taking is at least partially a matter of locus of control and tolerance for ambiguity. By becoming more self-aware through identifying the values that comprise your code of conduct, you automatically will feel increasing confidence in your decisions and more in control of your actions under conditions of ambiguity.

Your courage to take risk increases because of increasing confidence that you are doing the right thing. You have become self-empowered and in control of achieving success in any endeavor in which you may be involved. Sure, others may feel that you have failed. Nevertheless, you will know that you were doing the right thing and recover relatively fast from any result short of total success. Empowerment is necessary for all organizations. However, empowerment is not just a matter of your boss providing you with the discretion to make decisions without asking permission from some higher authority. The self provides the real strength to empower.

Self-awareness gives you the empowerment you needed. It is the internal locus of control you need to have the courage and confidence to take the risks needed to go beyond what you know and begin to explore the unknown. You are now out of the box and navigating based on who you are. You are in your own skin and it feels good.

THE ROLE OF INTUITION

The truly effective leader uses their own rules for thinking and action rather than rely on the rules that others would like us to follow. It is now not just okay to rely on our intuition, it has become a necessity to exercise our free will as we work our way out of the box.

Do not drive by your wake.
(Navy maxim)

Without our scientific methods, how are we going to make choices, what actions should we take? How do we predict outcomes or improve our understanding of human behavior?

DECISION-MAKING

Even decision theoretic models fall short of usefulness. In general, we typically would start our decision-making by a statement of the problem and identification of the outcomes of interest. However, when we consider ambiguity, we cannot even observe that a problem exists or what outcome we are trying to predict, understand, explain and control. How can we build any criterion model that would be useful under the conditions of ambiguity? The marketplace seems to thrive on the next new everything.

That little word "new" means that we are continuously challenged to deal with the unknown and the unknown is where ambiguity lives. Whenever we learn something new, we have moved into the realm of ambiguity. When a boss asks you what you will decide in some challenging situation, and your answer is "I don't know" you have entered the ambiguity zone.

In Figure 7, I have provided a summary of the decision methods (Hogarth, 1987. (Tversky & Kahneman, 1981; Tversky, & Kahneman. (1986). Salas & Cannon-Bower, 1996. Klein, Orasanu, Calderwood, & Zsambok, 1993; Kahneman, Slovic & Tversky, 1982; Perrin, Barnett, Walrath & Grossman, 2001) typically used under various conditions.

Three questions are considered: has the situation been encountered, or not encountered, has the problem been resolved or unresolved, and is there adequate time and resources.

However, this model does not consider ambiguity. If you acknowledge the possibility of an ambiguous basis for reality, then, the decision-making behaviors change drastically.

The graphic in Figure 7 indicates that: 1) when a decision situation is unencountered and unresolved the individual will search for expert model templates that can be applied in making a decision; 2) when the decision situation is one that the decision maker has encountered in the past and there was a successful outcome the decision maker will use personally experienced based templates to formulate a decision; 3) when the decision situation is one that has been encountered in the past and has been satisfactorily resolved, the results of standard experimental research methodologies are used; 4) when the situation can be characterized as never encountered (not encountered) and unresolved, then intuitive insight, pattern recognition, and improvisation is used.

FIGURE 7
DECISION SITUATION

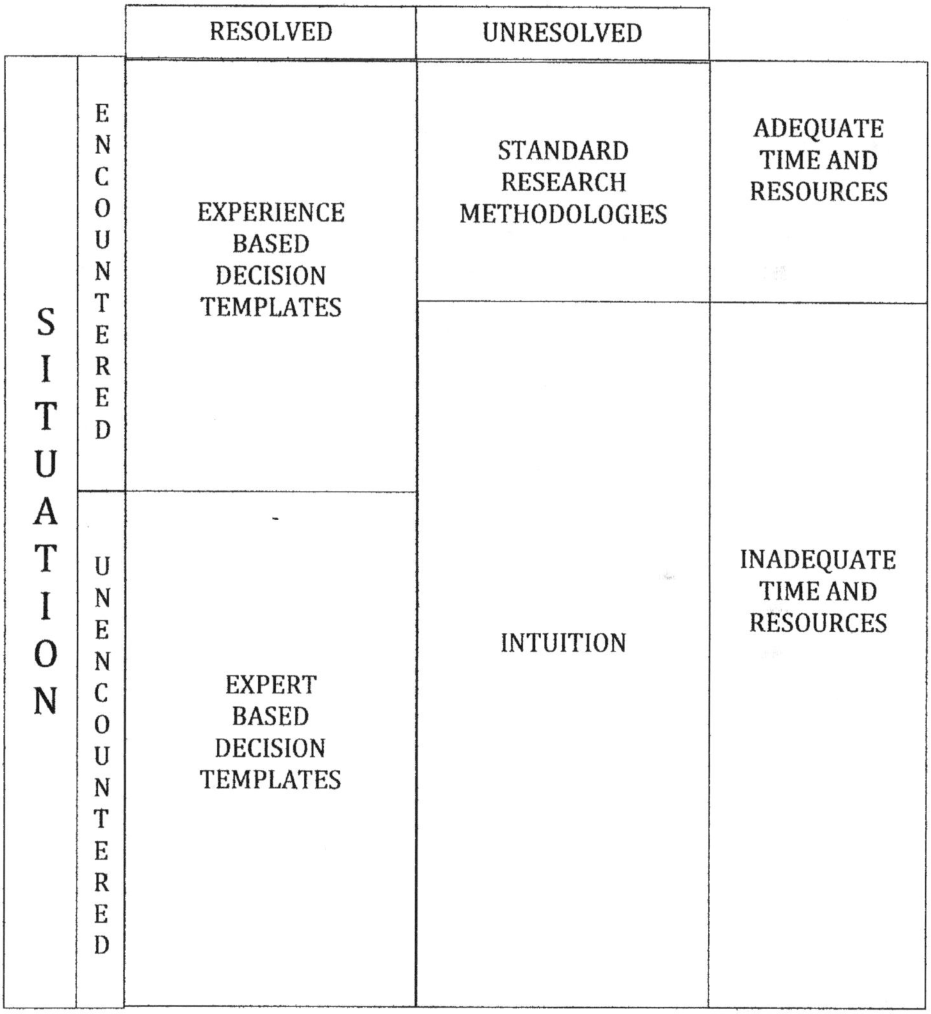

		RESOLVED	UNRESOLVED	
S **I** **T** **U** **A** **T** **I** **O** **N**	E N C O U N T E R E D	EXPERIENCE BASED DECISION TEMPLATES	STANDARD RESEARCH METHODOLOGIES	ADEQUATE TIME AND RESOURCES
	U N E N C O U N T E R E D	EXPERT BASED DECISION TEMPLATES	INTUITION	INADEQUATE TIME AND RESOURCES

These statements regarding ambiguity and normative decision-making models are appropriate for all situations involving human behavior. In addition, all of the cells in the graphic are subject to the error which bias introduces. It should come as no big surprise that my preference is to error on the side of personal bias that may be introduced by intuition. I am much more comfortable making decisions that reflect my personal bias than another's bias.

Let us face it, much of our acquired human capital is bias, and companies make hiring decisions based on a "fit" of an individual's bias with the organization's culture and objectives.

Decision makers typically consider reality as being uncertain and will not or do not acknowledge the possibility of ambiguity. When you consider that techniques appropriate under uncertain conditions is nearly all we learned, it would be a good guess that it would be hard to find ambiguous paradigms taught at any level within our educational systems.

The uncertainty-based methods of decision-making are useful in providing a way of thinking about models or templates for making decisions. In addition, descriptive and inferential statistics can be useful for fine-tuning our intuitive understandings. However, once you begin to think that quantitative techniques provide truth, you make a huge mistake. The quantitative probability based techniques are only useful for organizing our thinking when operating in the known. If, as many suggest, we are continually dealing with the unknown in business and life, we had better start developing our intuitive potentials. Yes, the unknown is uncomfortable, precisely because of ambiguity. Learning is difficult and it can be almost impossible if we do not build our tolerance for ambiguity and our intuitive skills.

Let me present two examples, which I believe may help clarify my present position. The first example considers the errors present under each model of decision-making.

One example uses slow thinking to represent experimentation and fast thinking to represent the other three models of decision-making (personal templates, expert templates, and intuition). I will use a classic example to counter the argument that "slow" thinking, analysis is superior to intuitive "fast" thinking.

The following example involves the extensive analysis that went into the design of the not so successful Edsel automobile. This was not "slow" thinking's finest hour. The Edsel's most memorable design feature was its trademark "horse-collar grille," which was quite distinct from other cars of the period. A popular joke at the time was that the Edsel "resembled an Oldsmobile sucking a lemon".

An additional intriguing aspect of the Edsel story is that it provides a case study in how a company's political bias can kill an idea. While the car and Ford's planning of the car are the most often cited reasons for its failure, internal Ford Motor Company memoranda suggest that the Edsel may actually have been a victim of dissension within Ford's management ranks. Robert McNamara wanted to "kill" the Edsel and he used his corporate political power to do it by eliminating the Edsel marketing budget. This is a good example of how political winds shifting over time, which may act against a particular decision being successful. My point is that the extensive analysis or "slow thinking" may not have been the reason for the failure of the Edsel. It was not the failure of the analysis that leads to the demise of the Edsel. It was the change in key personnel and the bias of political ideologies.

A contemporary example is the Scion Xb. People said that the car was funny looking and looked like a "toaster," not a car. Of course, the subsequent success of the Scion Xb, resulted in many competing automobile manufacturers deciding to copy many of the Scion Xb design features. We have many manufacturers of toasters on the highways today. They are called mini SUV's.

Another possibility is that other changes may occur which affect any initial judgments regarding the success or failure of a decision over time. Classic car collectors have decided that the Edsel has become a highly collectible item among vintage car hobbyists. Fewer than 10,000 Edsels survive and are now valuable collectors' items. A mint 1958-1960 convertible can sell at auction for over $100,000.

To summarize what might have happened: Maybe there was a great deal of analysis that went into the design or "slow" thinking. Maybe the grille was an intuitive decision or "fast" thinking. In addition, after the car was introduced McNamara did everything he could to make sure the Edsel failed. Finally, in the long-term collectors have found the Edsel to be a great success. All of these factors presented cognitive limitations in the decision making process that I agree would certainly add to the complexity of the decision situation.

However, many different factors impinge on the success or failure of a decision over time. Decisions, which led to the production of the Edsel, may have been initially the right decision, but changing organizational politics may have led to the Edsel's subsequent failure, and finally, vintage car collectors may argue that the Edsel was ultimately a success.

I find in this example that it would be difficult to sort out the influences of slow thinking, fast thinking, politics, or the temporal dynamic and bias. I feel that we could all come up with other examples of success or failure, which can be attributed to slow thinking, fast thinking, politics, or market whim. It should be clear by now that it is difficult, if not impossible, to measure success or failure of any single decision made at an earlier point in time. Bias is among the many difficulties we encounter when making any decision. I do not have a good grip on how to think about this, but only to say "isn't that the point". I find it a bit humorous when people refer to bias. I do not know if ambiguity creates the bias, or if bias creates ambiguity. Is not our bias an exercise in free will? Moreover, then, I ask, is there something wrong with free will.

Perhaps the following example will help clarify my point that every decision model has its limitation. While teaching at the Naval Postgraduate School I participated in some projects dealing with the effect of increases in compensation on the supply of high mental category recruits. The economists produced their models which indicated something like a 10% to 20% increase in the supply of high mental category recruits as compensation was increased.

The Admirals responded that they "didn't want to turn the military into "just" another job where money was the primary factor inducing enlistment diminishing the patriotic motive. They lost that fight to the politicians who decided to go full steam ahead into the volunteer force.

Now, it could be argued that the admirals "bias" should have ruled the day. Today we are moving closer to a quasi-mercenary military force. Then again, something may happen and the draft will come back and we will never know if the all-volunteer force was a success or not.

My point is that maybe any bias is as good as any other bias if you cannot agree on how success is measured. I am certain that there were many economists that felt the Admirals were foolish or, at least, naive in their thinking that patriotism was somehow important.

However, what were the Admirals to do when patriotism cannot be measured, and supply can be measured by simply counting. Even though, we might not know what we are counting because we need to first decide how we measure the quality of a recruit.

QUANTUM LEADERSHIP

Intuition is not a thought process. Quite the opposite, intuition is not thinking at all. Let me explain. In the Buddhist, tradition intuition is regarded as the mindfulness phenomenon. It is easy to misunderstand the meaning of mindfulness. The mind is not full in the sense that it contains everything and requires intense concentration on understanding reality. Actually, it is more like the "no mind."

Think of the mind as a clean blackboard with absolutely nothing on it. Eliminate all preconceived notions of reality. Next in more of a wishful state than concentration, you permit the reality of the moment to occupy or fill up the empty mind (the blackboard). It is important to note here that self-awareness is necessary for the reality of the moment to find its way into your total being.

Intuition or gut feeling is an instantaneous knowing of what needs to be done. It creates heroes, visionaries, and amazingly inspirational and charismatic leaders. It is a doing without any conscious intellectual decision process. Artists and scientists alike as well as athletes know that intuition is real because they may have been lucky enough to experience it.

In athletics, it is being "in the zone." In fact, the mindfulness technique is a common approach that abstract artists rely upon in creating a particular artwork. The abstract or existential artist certainly could not be as creative as they are if they had to think about what they were doing and plan things out first. For the scientist, it may be known as the "ah ha" moment.

All artistic and probably the greatest scientific endeavors involve what might be known as the no mind or empty mind experience. None of these experiences is thought of as knowing what to do, but simply what to do is known and choice is enacted by taking action in the moment, without thinking.

Once a problem or opportunity has presented itself all external stimuli, pose a potential distraction to the empty mind. The empty mind is one's self-awareness that is providing the template or "eyes" for the complete unconscious focus for action in the moment and things can seem to go into slow motion or at least for the unconscious focus of the mind, time essentially stands still and the patterns in the chaos come more clearly into practical focus.

Our self-awareness provides the confidence needed to enter into the mindfulness state of unconscious focus without allowing external stimuli to become any distraction. Mindfulness is not very comfortable without confidence and almost any distraction can become a large obstacle to making decisions based on the no mind. Any stimuli, which are negative from the perspective of the internal values of self, can disrupt this intuitive mindful state of internal/external focus. It is during this internal focus of thought any naysayers be kept away from the intuitive leader. In fact, they need to voluntarily or involuntarily leave the organization altogether because they are what I refer to as the "intuition assassins." They can kill intuitive potentials of the individual or organization.

Intuition is very fast decision-making. It is acting as if you already know and have envisioned the results and all that remains is to create the results you see. Intuitive leadership is simply creating what we already know. (Gloor, 2011; Cappon, 1994; Bennis, Spreitzer, Cummings, 2001; Williams, 1998; Mitchell, Friga, & Mitchell, 2005; Parker, & Begnaud, 2004)

The intuitive person does not have to think about theories, alternatives, or analysis of collected data. Intuitive people simply act on an understanding of their relationship to everything around them, which is made possible by self-awareness. An intuitive uses their self-awareness as a balance point between arbitrary externally provided biases and the constant bias of personal values.

It is important to realize that intuition is not fortune telling and the future is not predestined to occur. Therefore, in a way intuition is seeing the alternative futures and taking action in the moment to create the future you want. In addition, intuitive leadership is not necessarily just one person. It may actually be referring to a collective of people. So, teams or organizations can be thought of as having intuitive leadership. Building intuitive leadership potential within the entire organization is the ideal objective.

Self-awareness is the key that opens the door to being intuitive. Intuition or foresight cannot occur without first having become self-aware. Not only must the intuitive leader be self-aware, but they must also be aware of others' self-awareness plus the relationships among all stimuli in the overall environmental context.

The intuitive leader has reached the highest degree of confidence and is motivated by intrinsic rewards received from intuitive performance.

Intuition is unencumbered by the distraction of rules, codes or principles expressed by others and rational thought.

Intuition allows navigating through the turbulence of our times and not blindly driving by one's wake using empirical methods. When you do not just understand what to do, but also, know why to do it, our foresight is improved. We are not interested in the patterns in the chaos that existed in the past. We are interested in applying what we know to seeing the patterns in the current moment and how alternative futures may result.

Intuition is imperative because conscious reasoning, analysis, logic, and science are too limited even for daily use. Scientists make no apology about the limits that the scientific method places on our judgment and free will. Science, when used mechanistically, does inhibit free will.

Quantum physics states that there are not only material things that are real but something else that we cannot see called "form" or "string entanglement" that defines the infinite potential of nature and is equally real. These waveforms determine the connectedness that creates material things.

The weather provides a simplified illustration of reality being a combination of particles and waves. If we were to think of a tornado as the particle (the seen reality) and the pattern of the high and low-pressure fronts as the waves (unseen reality), we can see that the action of the tornado is not a matter of the tornado itself, but, the changing wave patterns. The infinite potential is contained in the movement of the waves that make up the storm front. These patterns or relationships, not the material things are what provide us with an intuitive understanding of each moment.

The forecast or understanding of an outcome (where the tornado is going) is predicted by the waves that created the storm itself. If, as in materialist Newtonian physics we were to define reality through measurement of the material things, our reality would be a deception. A quantum view of reality considers both the particles' and the waves' potentials.

The "Quantum Leader" understands the importance of insight about self and foresight about the future reality and the potentials that are unseen. You cannot prove through measurement that every mind is connected to some kind of cosmic mind. You can only prove it to yourself. This proof is apparent, only when the individual is self-aware. This self-awareness (memories) is our coded reason for our existence. The cosmic spirit or quantum reality finds you. However, there must first be a "you." The cosmic mind can find you only when you are self-aware and listening.

The self-awareness that we discover within our memories is like the hard wiring of a cosmic receiver that allows the universal consciousness to communicate to us an understanding of a cosmic perspective of reality. This cosmic reality expresses the infinite potential of the cosmic mind. It is this understanding of reality that forms our potential for intuition. The universal consciousness is difficult to understand, but even neuroscientists have reached the point of defining consciousness as the processing of information within a system. The fascinating thing is that everything processes information at the quantum level. Our reality can then be seen as the result of the universal consciousness and the sensing of the connectedness of all the information systems, which exist in all things.

Very early in his scientific career, Bohm trusted this interior, intuitive display as a more reliable way of arriving at solutions to very complex problems. Later, when he met Einstein, he learned that Einstein also experienced subtle, internal muscular sensations that appeared to lie much deeper than ordinary rational and discursive thought. Without knowing it, Bohm had returned to an ancient maxim "as above, so below". In other words, this maxim teaches us that each individual is the microcosm of the macrocosm.

Bohm himself strongly believed he was part of the universe and that, by giving attention to his own feelings and sensations, he should be able to arrive at a deeper understanding of the nature of the universe.

The ability to experience processes at the muscular, sensory level was with him for his entire life. It was not so much that Bohm visualized a physical system as that he was able to sense its dynamics within his body: He had the feeling that internally he could experience the analogy of the solution to the problem he was considering. (Peate, 1996)

Intuition is imperative to any study of human behavior and certainly any situation that might be defined as ambiguous. It is easier to put a man on the moon or to produce the miracles of modern technology than it is to predict the subtle or not so subtle ambiguities of the marketplace or human behavior in organized settings.

Making decisions under ambiguous conditions requires the decision maker to evaluate alternative actions. However, how can we evaluate alternatives when we do not know the outcome or it cannot be measured? This is precisely where self-awareness comes into play. Our values are what we use in the evaluation of the characteristics of each alternative. The abstract ultimate outcome (that cannot be measured directly) is evaluated by each alternative solution as it is filtered through our values.

Think back to the Admirals concern about the all-volunteer military. They were using their value for patriotism to evaluate whether increasing pay to attract sufficient recruits was the right alternative. The economists were using money as the primary value in determining how the supply of recruits would be affected as defined by the supply of recruits based on pay increases. Gun control, the right to life, violence in the media, taxing the rich, and immigration are all examples of the use of different values in the regulation of individual behavior.

If the boundary of strict science is placed somewhere between biology and physics, then, when it comes to sociology, psychology, economics and the liberal arts, we have little choice, we must become more intuitive and so too must our leaders. We first gain insight from self-awareness and then develop foresight with our intuitive self. We have ample proof that most of the living to be done is not susceptible to scientific predictive precision.

Our intuitive feeling self is the holographic and instantaneous understanding of our world. Self-awareness is the template that provides our intense internal focus on the situation at hand. (See Figure 8)

FIGURE 8
SELF-AWARENESS – INTUITION –
ACTION IN THE MOMENT

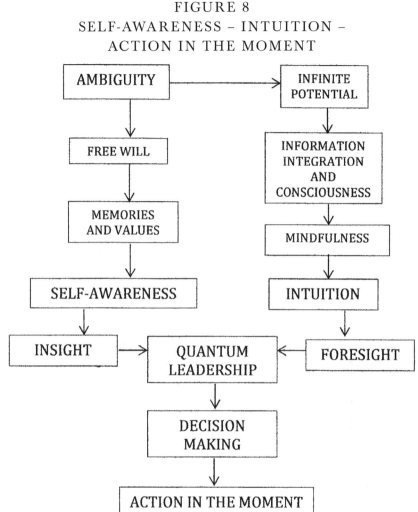

Intuition is the internal rule maker in your life. Externally confirmed rules no longer have much meaning for who we are. Research on video games has actually confirmed that 1) when games are based on internally confirmed rules, the game requires greater attention, results in greater learning and greater satisfaction with the game than when the rules are externally supported. Remember experiences most of us had of pure play when we simply got together and made up the rules of the game as we played. Well, it is a good deal like that.

Today, turbulent, ever altering, and threatening environments make it imperative to resolve problems and to avoid hazards proactively. By the time we react, it might be too late. Therefore, we need the full complement of intuitive skills in order to tackle proactively the main problems of the day. There is no logical way to encounter the unknown. Intuition allows us to think beyond the superficial appearance of situations and events. We happen to live in a place where the unknown just barely reveals itself to the known. Entering the unknown requires a great deal of imagination and imagination is essentially a process of making up or changing the rules.

Intuition is seeing the forest in the trees. It is holographic reasoning that is consistent with whom you are and is very effective when the situation is ambiguous. It involves instantaneous consideration of everything that may impinge on the results of any action. Our action in the moment is the balance between self-awareness or insight about self and intuition or foresight regarding various states of the future and what will happen. It might be said that improvisation is intuition in action.

Progressive educators are now developing improvisation games and exercises in grade school so that children will begin developing the skills needed to deal with ambiguity in life. An important consideration is that we are all agents in the creation of the future. It is not that intuition is seeing a predetermined future. It is acknowledging that we can influence the future and take the action that will realize our vision of the future.

This is the intuition that reveals itself in the gut feeling we have about what may result in the future. We refer to this as the gut feeling simply because there is no apparent reason behind the feeling that could explain why we feel we must do something for which there can be no clear explanation for doing some particular thing.

It is our feeling regarding the correct action based on who we are and how we must act in the moment to make the future we want. We must not live in the past or the future.

A decision based on intuition also tends to maximize contingency plans and simultaneously consider all the possible outcomes of a decision and subsequent options which are available if or when each alternative outcome may result. Good chess players and poker players are often quite good at this, as are coaches in various sporting activities. The great coaches can "feel" when the team is in the zone and will let them play on without changing the game plan. These coaches know how fragile the empty mind team play is and any change can take the team out of the zone. When a team naturally is "in the zone" and any change made in players or tactics, being "in the zone" will disappear and it is very difficult to regain it, no matter how hard you might try.

The second subtlety is one that reflects that doing nothing is one possible action. This can be expressed by the following principle. If it is <u>not</u> necessary that you make a decision, it is necessary that you <u>do not</u> make a decision. I have personally found this principle quite useful and sometimes it may be the best alternative response to a very ambiguous situation. It is a feeling that even though for many people the situation may be impossible you get a feeling that if you leave the situation alone, the problem may resolve itself. This means that sometimes you must realize that you are not and cannot be the "wizard" and control everything. Sometimes the situation rather has its own destiny. It is something like; if it is not broken do not fix it. If the situation will resolve itself in your favor, leave it alone. Sometimes you may have to wait for another moment when action will make a difference.

We need to take action in the moment as illustrated by the following examples of the use of intuition. Consider the basketball player on a fast break that passes the ball successfully behind his back to a teammate without even looking. This is acting in the moment or in the zone.

The player passing the ball wasn't thinking, but simply self-aware and knowing what can be done without thinking (i.e. The patterns in the chaos of the fast break) to reach the outcome of interest (scoring). We see this intuitive action most often in athletics because so many people are watching and in awe of what they are seeing.

Intuition and "the empty mind" is also seen on the battlefield when we see unthinking heroism and it also happens every day in businesses everywhere when action without thinking is critical. It is also perhaps one of the reasons when a hero is interviewed, they shy away from being called a hero precisely because they acted in an unthinking manner in the moment and don't feel they have acted heroically. This is an excellent example of the empty mind concept in Buddhist teachings.

We have been taught that the best decision is made by careful deliberation of all the facts and then select the best alternative to enact. The athlete and the intuitive leader know they do not have the luxury of having time to analyze the situation. We need to let our self-awareness and intuition drive our instantaneous decision-making.

If life knocks you down, self-awareness and the consequent integrity help you get back up and regain your balance. Your intuitive abilities provide the simultaneous foresight and confidence needed to enact your vision. Intuition does not guarantee success. However, you can maintain confidence under threatening conditions and continue to navigate when things are dark and threatening. You are inspired by self and others are inspired by your integrity when making decisions. I think it is human nature to seek out inspiration. Nevertheless, even those who are not originally inspired by who you are will, over time, almost without noticing, find themselves inspired.

The success in using your intuition includes your ability to manipulate the external environment to ensure that the results will be positive. Because others are on the same page, they too act to ensure that the results are positive. So good outcomes of a decision may not be directly attributed to an abstract concept of intuition, per se, but indirectly to your own and others inspiration and the manipulation of the environment, moment to moment, to ensure success. Intuition includes as much the "willing" of a future and inspiring others to pursue the vision of the leader. We have all heard it stated that if you can see it, you can make it happen.

Once everyone in the organization becomes more self-aware and can identify who they are, in terms of the values that guide their action, it then becomes important that these values be shared and the organization itself can then move toward their vision for themselves or the organization's vision. As the organization achieves self-awareness and develops a shared set of values there are two very critical outcomes that result. First, as indicated previously, deceit is eliminated and mutual trust grows. Second, everyone is more confident, not just in themselves, but also with others in the organization. This confidence becomes the basis for the growth of both self and others.

Trust and respect is the foundation for any strong culture. Without trust and respect, the culture becomes toxic and susceptible to any challenge. Self-awareness plus trust and respect is the basic formula for the development of not just a culture, but also a strong culture that can withstand external threats.

The objective is not that there should be a consensus of values throughout the organization, only that values become transparent across the organization. There is no set of values that must be applied universally, only that a kind of value architecture becomes transparent across the organization. The expression of these values makes it possible to identify an understanding of the why behind everyone's decisions and action. This architectural understanding is the organizational culture. It is the basis for cooperation and coordination of operations in achieving concerted action toward the achievement of organizational objectives and the enactment of the organization's vision. You have become an organization with a strong culture. The organization itself has now become self-aware. The organization is in the zone.

Having already discovered the self we now have our inspiration. This inspiration takes the form of the vision one has for self and the organization, as well as, the organization's culture. We may now passionately live our lives to the fullest extent and we will always know what to do.

Not only do our lives have meaning, but also we can share who we are with others through our stories of what we value and our current actions. Others in the organization recognize who you are and respect what they see you do. Others will know why we act the way we do and they understand that if we are acting in opposition to who we truly are, then, when confronted by this inconsistent behavior we will change. Others can actually help ensure that we are living our reason for being. And, not only that, but we can help others discover their being so they may share with others and we can help ensure they are living their life, self-aware and moving continually to the organization's vision by enacting a very strong culture.

The culture of the organization unfolds as we all enact our newly found and shared self-awareness. The leader can mold an organization with others who are inspired by the vision for the company.

Truly visionary people and organizations are also distinguished by a high degree of emotional intelligence, which requires self-awareness. The results of your decisions will leave a legacy behind. This legacy embraces your personal vision and also the organization vision and culture. Organizational leaders are the guardians of organization culture. Others in the organization look up to the leader as the role model that exemplifies the organization's reason for existence.

As employees follow the organizational leaders they become empowered, inspired and the culture continues to grow stronger. The leader must take great care to not betray the organization's vision. They have become the keystone of the organization. Forgetting about the organization's vision and culture is like destroying the immune system of the organization and it may die from a simple cold. It does not take long for the organization to tumble into ruin. It takes a strong leader to turn this situation around if it can be.

Self-awareness of values is different from goals. The values form the foundation for judgment and action in the development of tactics and strategy in the attainment of organizational growth and sustainability. Ultimately, decisions must first consider the values that give reason for our existence and only after consideration of self can organization policy, tactics, and strategy lead to organizational effectiveness and continual progress toward the organization's vision. The effects of self-awareness on organizational outcomes, along with trust and re-spect lead to the confidence needed to be creative and innovative and therefore the learning and consequently the continual improvement needed to achieve organizational effectiveness as the organization itself becomes self-aware.

SUMMARY

I have attempted to explain why we have many of the problems we face today. The basic reason is that we have ignored reality. We have been developing behavioral theories on an assumed reality that are based on uncertainty

When we accept ambiguity as the determining characteristic of reality, everything changes. Being self-aware and the procedure of becoming self-aware become critical to the successful operation of an organization and its members. Communication and team effectiveness subsequently are enhanced and visionary, intuitive leaders may emerge, and a very high level of integrity is attained.

The result is an architectural understanding of the values that make us who we are and the culture and inspired visions of the future become clearer. Identifying the values that provide us with how we comprehend the cosmos around us is of overriding importance. These values are revealed by exploring our unforgettable memories. The unforgettable memories are unforgettable because of the values that are expressed by these profound experiences. They supply us with a vivid experiential portrayal of who we are and how we see ourselves as we enact our reality.

These memories provide the key to the discovery of your values and becoming self-aware. Self-awareness subsequently results in trust, respect, empowerment, communication effectiveness, team cohesiveness, strong culture, intuitive leadership, continual improvement, and overall organizational effectiveness. Yes, self-awareness is the key to how an organization functions in almost every way.

A story might be useful to illustrate the connections between ambiguity, self-awareness, and intuitive leadership. It was 1995 or 1996 and I had organized a course of travel/study for a group of students for a business opportunity tour that I designed for college credit. The class traveled to Vietnam to study the process of identifying business opportunities in a rapidly growing economy in a developing country. Prior to leaving, we met several times to prepare for the prospect of culture shock that may arise during our travels.

The streets in Vietnam are some of the busiest I had ever seen in all my travels. There are seven million people in Ho Chi Minh City and it actually seems like there are fourteen million motorcycles on the streets. After adding a cacophony of sound produced by trucks, bicycles, taxis and pedestrians crossing the street everywhere, it appeared and sounded even smelled quite chaotic. Getting across the street can be described as extremely ambiguous. There was no way to plan how you would go about crossing the street.

Vietnamese navigated this chaos quite readily. They would look for the first bit of space immediately off the curb and would take the first step out in the traffic and then would look for the next open space that would move them another step to the other side of the street and would proceed one step at a time to cross the street to the other side, one step at a time. There was very little time between the steps and it did not take long for them to cross the street seemingly unaware of the chaos around them. The traffic moved around the individual like the water in a stream moving around a boulder as the traffic moved around the individual and the individual moved through the traffic.

On the other hand, the American would typically stand on one side of the street and look for an opportunity or a gap in the traffic that would allow them to dash quickly from one side to the other. Of course, as the story goes, the American never makes it to the other side. Americans take much too long in preparation for the perfect moment. The past is no longer useful and we do not have a clue of what will happen in the future. You have to be "in the moment" to know what to do. This story was one of the best teaching moments in our preparation to travel to Vietnam.

The class also allowed each student to share experiences that stood out in their memories and quickly developed into a very cohesive group that individually and collectively was growing more self-aware by sharing the unforgettable moments that reflected their values. As it happened, when we moved as a group across streets in Vietnam we all recalled the story and to my surprise our entire group, like a scrum, of twelve students and two professors found ourselves moving effortlessly across the streets one step at a time. We also did not even think about our movement, we just knew how to get across the street. It was not that one of us was calling out instructions of when we were to move.

We all moved at once even with no leader taking charge. It was surreal. I remember thinking after we had crossed the street, how did we do that? We also developed quite a bit of trust and respect for each other and became very confident in our relationship with a very different culture than our own. We acknowledged that we were going to experience a great amount of ambiguity. Moreover, we dealt with it every day. We had increased our self-awareness in identifying and sharing stories each of us had stored in our memories. We had become comfortable with relying on each other because of our trust and respect that we had for each other. Finally, we had become very comfortable with relying upon our intuition instead of rigid planning. We realized that every moment could present a surprise.

I deliberately use "we" and not "I" because I was not some great leader that shouted out instructions. At least not as leadership is conventionally understood. Self-awareness and intuition had become a substitute for leadership in the traditional sense. The intuitive leader is the individual or group that creates and protects the total system and culture. This comfort with our intuitive selves proved useful in many ways during our travels because everything, every day was ambiguous and very chaotic. It was a trip loaded with teaching moments and the students were happy with their learning experience beyond my expected learning outcomes. Actually, we achieved much less of what I had planned, and much more of what the group wanted as our experiences unfolded. I "gave them their heads," we all adapted, and learning was enhanced. Our internal rules for action, not external rules, guided our action.

I hope that this story not only helps clarify some of the conceptual relationships provided in this book, but also demonstrates how subtle the effects of ambiguity, self-awareness, and intuition are in our everyday experiences. (See Figure 9)

FIGURE 9
GRAPHIC SUMMARY MODEL

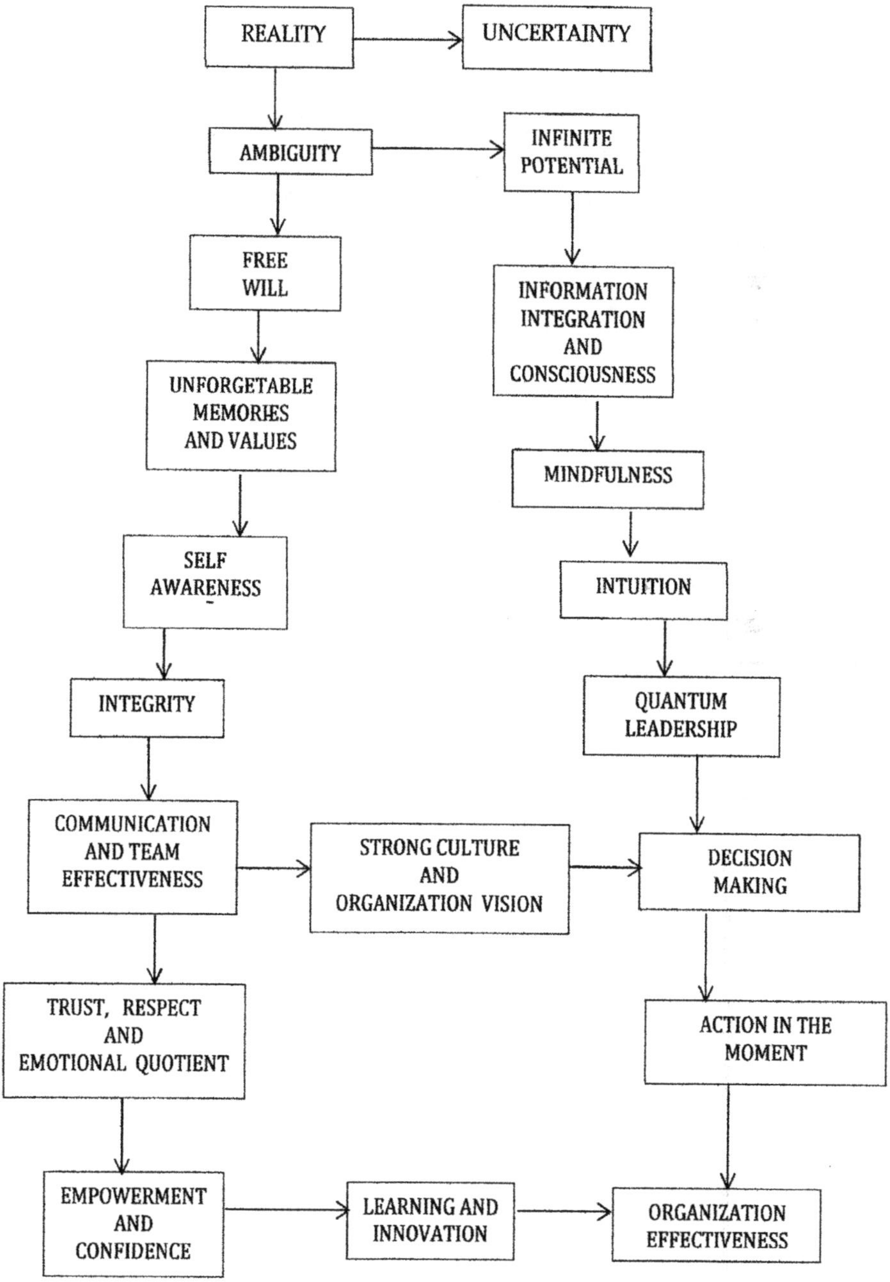

When uncertainty is the assumed reality of today's mega-corporation, the organization tends to move toward the development of the organization along the lines of a machine. This mechanistic characteristic of the typical big business enterprise fails to anticipate peoples' problems and human reactions to crises. Organizations are constantly, moving from what they think is known into the unknown, and there will inevitably be unanticipated people problems and organization crises. Ambiguity is present in these business environments.

Often the typical large mechanistic organization will make errors that are the result of unethical decisions. The machine does not recognize that the unknown never before encountered problems do not fit nicely within the machine's coded parameters. The machine tries to respond to the ambiguous, unknown and ultimately becomes corrupt. We are all familiar with the corruption of many businesses or governments that occupies today's news headlines.

Corporate board members need to get real and confront ambiguity. It really is a matter of knowing what to do when it happens and it is what happens in the next moment that may be the most important moment in our development. Leadership is not a role assigned to an individual. Leadership is a set of functions that is the responsibility of everyone in the organization.

BUSINESSES PUSH BACK

There are many aspects of what I have presented that could be challenged and certainly will be and perhaps even should be. Over the years, I have shared the views presented here with students, business executives, government officials, and academic colleagues. All of them agreed with me and felt that something was wrong with the way we think and make decisions.

Generally, they would nod their agreement, smile, and tell me something like, "If I presented your position to my superiors, they would probably at the very least, laugh me out of the room or worse, they would dismiss me, even, for bringing up such an absurd idea. When I asked them why? They would offer the following types of arguments in opposition to my position. The responsibility of business is to maximize profit through the production and distribution of goods and services in a market exchange. This is the main principle of a capitalistic economy.

The following represents additional arguments they would typically offer:

1. The job of business is business, and everything else is a distraction from the goal of maximizing stakeholder value.

2. Using business resources (capital or labor) for other purposes lessens the amount available for the business's economic mission and is thus an act of irresponsibility to society and be claimed as unethical.

3. Business managers who divert business resources from profit maximization are stealing from owners and not fulfilling their duty to them. (They were actually, with a straight face, saying that it is unethical to be ethical.)

4. Business managers lack the inclination, training, and skills to understand and offer answers to ethical problems.

5. If the vast resources and power of businesses were used to implement business solutions to social problems, it would represent a major threat to democracy.

6. Global and industrial competition makes ethical problems luxuries that businesses can no longer afford.

7. The drive for short-term profits makes it difficult or impossible for businesses to be responsible for anything other than economic and legal areas.

8. The machine structure of large corporations discourages business people from acting in ethically responsible ways.

When they would finish, I would generally say something like do you mean to say values such as human dignity, compassion, trust, respect, forgiveness, tolerance, equality, justice and humanity are antithetical to business because they have costs in a capitalistic society and are a distraction from the profit motive. Okay, so business is simply a well-oiled machine that is built to maximize profit for the good of society. Continuing, I would generally say something like, "Tell me I am wrong, but what you are actually saying is that choice based on free will doesn't enter into consideration." Oh, now I see, what is wrong with me?

Yes, eureka, the job of business is to convince people that business will take care of them. Oh, oh, and that means that if you placed like-minded people in government offices that were important to ensuring business success, business would be more successful. Then these officials would strategically appoint judges in the legal system and, with the excess profit generated, society would be better off.

My position is that we must admit that ambiguity is fundamental to our existence, become more self-aware, celebrate risk taking, fearlessly enter the unknown, and develop the potentials of intuitive leadership. We do not have the time to take the easy way out by thinking of building reality based on uncertainty and allowing probabilities to fatalistically run our lives.

We clearly have much to do. It certainly is time for the next paradigm shift. We need to develop an understanding of how to find patterns in the chaos and take "Action in the Moment."

I hope this book encourages a serious conversation about the assumptions we make about reality, and how important self-awareness and intuition are in responding to the apparent chaos presented by ambiguity. At least we need to recognize that we really cannot know much about our own behavior until we understand the reason we exist. Just think about it because the reason for our existence is the key that unlocks the door to our future.

> *"Man must not attempt to dispel the ambiguity of his being*
> *but, on the contrary, accept the task of realizing it."*
> Simone de Beauvoir, The Ethics of Ambiguity, As cited in Guignon,
> Charles, The Good Life, Hackett Publishing, Inc., 1999,p263.
> Accessed from https://books.google.com

BIBLIOGRAPHY

Beebe, J. Integrity in Depth. (1992). Texas A&M University Press, College Station, TX.

Bennis, W., Spreitzer, G., Cummings, T.(2001). The Future Of Leadership Today's Top Leadership Thinkers Speak to Tomorrow's Leaders, Jossey-Bass, San Francisco.

Brooks, D. (2015). The Road to Character, Random House, New York

Buck, M. A. (2004). Mentoring: A Promising Strategy for Creating and Sustaining a Learning Organization. Adult Learning.

Byers, W. (2010). How Mathematicians Think: Using Ambiguity, Contradiction, and Paradox to Create Mathematics. Princeton, NJ: Princeton University Press.

Cady, S. H., Wheeler, J. V., DeWolf, J., & Brodke, M. (2011). Mission, Vision, and Values: What Do They Say? Organization Development Journal, 29 (1), 63+.

Cappon, D. (1994). Intuition and Management: Research and Application. Westport, CT: Quorum Books.

Dalla Costa, J. (1998). The Ethical Imperative: Why Moral Leadership Is Good Business. Reading, MA: Perseus Publishing.

Einstein, A., As cited on URL http://www.goodreads.com/quotes/tag/intuition

Fang, S., & Wang, J. (2006). Effects of Organizational Culture and Learning on Manufacturing Strategy Selection: An Empirical Study. International Journal of Management, 23 (3), 503+.

Feibleman, J. K. (1962). Foundations of Empiricism. The Hague: Martinus Nijhoff.

Frost, Robert (2002). The Ethics of Ambiguity, Bucknell University Press, Lewisburg, PA.

Gloor, P. A. (2006). Swarm Creativity: Competitive Advantage through Collaborative Innovation Networks. New York: Oxford University Press.

Gloor, P. A. (2011, March/April). To Become a Better Manager Stop Being a Manager. Ivey Business Journal Online.

Graf, A. B., Jr. (2005, March). Building Corporate Cultures. Chief Executive (U.S.), (206), 18.

Hogarth, R. M. (1987). Judgment and choice (2nd ed.). New York: Wiley-Interscience.

Holbeche, L. (2011). GP Consortia: Navigating Ambiguity to Produce Greater Public Value? Perspectives in Public Health, 131 (3), 131+.

Jelinek, M., & Litterer, J. A. (1995). Toward Entrepreneurial Organizations: Meeting Ambiguity with Engagement. Entrepreneurship: Theory and Practice, 19 (3), 137+.

Kahneman, D., Slovic, P., & Tversky, A. (1982). Judgment under uncertainty: Heuristics and biases. New York: Cambridge University Press.

Klein, G. A., Orasanu, J., Calderwood, R., & Zsambok, C. E. (1993). Decision making in action: Models and methods. Norwood, NJ: Ablex.

Kruks, S. (2012). Simone de Beauvoir and the Politics of Ambiguity. New York: Oxford University Press.

Lynn, A. B. (2004). The EQ Difference: A Powerful Program for Putting Emotional Intelligence to Work. New York: AMACOM.

Mangham, I. (2004). 3: Leadership and Integrity. In J. Storey (Ed.), Leadership in Organizations: Current Issues and Key Trends (pp. 41-57). London: Routledge.

Marques, J. (2006). Leading the 21st Century Workplace: The Easy versus the Hard Part of Being an Awakened Leader. Business Renaissance Quarterly, 1 (3), 35+.

McKeown, E. (2010, November). Staying Current with the Nature of Work Is Critical. T&D, 64 (11), 21.

Mitchell, J. R., Friga, P. N., & Mitchell, R. K. (2005). Untangling the Intuition Mess: Intuition as a Construct in Entrepreneurship Research. Entrepreneurship Theory and Practice29, 6, 653–679.

Parker, J. P., & Begnaud, L. G. (2004). Developing Creative Leadership. Portsmouth, NH: Teacher Ideas Press.

Peate, David F., (1996), Infinite Potental, Helix Books, Addison-Wesley Publishing Company, Inc.

Perrin, B. M., Barnett, B. J., Walrath, L., & Grossman, J. D. (2001). Information order and outcome framing: An assessment of judgment bias in a naturalistic decision-making context. *Human Factors, 43,* 227–238.

Salas. E. & Cannon-Bowers, J. A. (Eds.). (1996). Decision making in complex environments [Special issue]. Human Factors, 38(2).

Schafer, Lothar (2013), Infinite Potential: What Quantum Physics Reveals About How We Should Live, Random House, Inc., New York.

Simone de Beauvoir, The Ethics of Ambiguity (1947), As cited in Guignon, Charles, The Good Life, Hackett Publishing, Inc., 1999, p263. Accessed from https://books.google.com.

Thorpe, W. H. (1956). Learning and Instinct in Animals. London: Methuen.

Tjan, A., Harrington, R. & Hsieh, T., (2012). Heart, Smarts, Guts, and Luck: What It Takes to Be an Entrepreneur and Build a Great Business, Harvard Business Review Press.

Tversky, A., & Kahneman, D. (1981). The framing of decisions and the psychology of choice. Science, 211, 453-458.

Tversky, A., & Kahneman, D.. (1986). Rational Choice and the Framing of Decisions. *The Journal of Business*, *59*(4), S251–S278. Retrieved from http://www.jstor.org/stable/2352759.

Williams, M. R. (1998). Mastering Leadership: Key Techniques for Managing and Leading a Winning Team. Thorogood, London.

Wright, Neill (1952) The Writing of Arabic Numerals (Publications of the Scottish Council for Research in Education, Volume XXXIII).

ABOUT THE AUTHOR

THOMAS G. SWENSON, Ph.D., earned his doctorate in management from the University of Oregon. His career has deviated from the traditional academic career. He has taught traditional aged and adult students, active U.S. and foreign military, government officials from Commonwealth, Central Asian and South Asian countries, members of royal  families and top government officials on the Arabian Peninsula, and business executives from various countries. He has guided the founding of English language centers and universities in foreign countries, and created his own startup apparel company in Vietnam. His career has had transitions driven by curiosity and inspired by the unknown in searching for the next unique challenge.

Printed in the United States
By Bookmasters